The Russian Revolution

usan Willoughby

Heinemann

Heinemann Educational,
a division of Heinemann Publishers (Oxford) Ltd,
Halley Court, Jordan Hill, Oxford OX2 8EJ

OXFORD LONDON EDINBURGH MADRID
ATHENS BOLOGNA PARIS MELBOURNE
SYDNEY AUCKLAND SINGAPORE TOKYO
IBADAN NAIROBI HARARE GABORONE
PORTSMOUTH NH (USA)

First published 1995

98 97 96 95 10 9 8 7 6 5 4 3 2 1

**British Library Cataloguing in Publication Data is
available from the British Library on request.**

ISBN 0–435–30926 9

Designed by Ron Kamen, Green Door Design Ltd,
Basingstoke

Illustrated by Jeff Edwards and Hardlines, Oxford

Printed in Spain by Mateu Cromo

The front cover shows Lenin leading the people, from a
contemporary Bolshevik poster.

Acknowledgements

The author and publisher would like to thank Oleag
Padalko for translating documents from Russian into
English. Also Valeri Silenko, Galina Ivanova and Vasilya
Ananiev for other original material.

The author and publisher would like to thank the
following for permission to reproduce photographs:

Illustrated London News: 3.19
Harlingue/Roger-Viollet, Paris: 5.5
Hulton Deutsch Collection: 1.6, 2.1, 3.5, 4.8, 6.2
David King Collection: 2.14, 3.2, 3.7, 4.2
Mansell Collection: 1.4, 3.1, 3.3
Lioudmila Protsai and Yuri Shelayev: 5.2, 5.3
Rex Features: 1.16
Society for Co-operation in Russian and Soviet Studies:
2.11, 4.4, 4.6, 4.9
Sovfoto, New York/Tass: Cover
Times Newspapers Ltd/Michael Powell: 1.12
Susan Willoughby: 4.1

Every effort has been made to contact copyright holders
of material published in this book. Any omissions will be
rectified in subsequent printings if notice is given to the
publisher.

*For Nadezhda Ananieva, her family and all my good
friends in Cherkassy, Ukraine.*

Details of written sources

In some sources the wording or sentence structure has
been simplified to ensure that the source is accessible.

Clare Baker, *Russia 1917–45*, Heinemann, 1990: 2.10,
3.9, 4.3, 4.5, 4.7
Heather Cubitt, *Russia under the last Tsar*, Longman,
1980: 2.3, 2.13
Tony Howarth, *Twentieth Century History: The World
since 1900*, Longman, 1979: 5.7, 5.8
Donald Mack, *Lenin and the Russian Revolution*,
Longman, 1970: 5.6
R. K. Massie, *Nicholas and Alexandra*, Gollancz, 1968:
1.2, 2.6
Sir Bernard Pares, *Fall of the Russian Monarchy*, Vintage
Books, 1971: 2.2, 2.4
Boris Pasternak, *Dr Zhivago*, Collins, 1958: 3.8, 5.4
Paul Shuter and Terry Lewis, *Skills in History 3*,
Heinemann, 1988: 3.4
Anthony Summers and Tom Mangold, *The File on the
Tsar*, Gollancz, 1976: 1.2, 1.3, 1.5, 1.7, 1.8, 1.9, 1.10, 1.11
John L. Taylor, *Russia in Revolution*, Holmes
McDougall, 1974: 2.15, 2.17, 3.6
Alan White, *Russia and the USSR 1905 to 1964*, Collins
Educational, 1994: 2.8
Alan Wood, *The Origins of the Russian Revolution*,
Lancaster Pamphlets, Routledge, 1993: 2.12

Note

In this book some of the words are printed in **bold**
type. This indicates that the word is listed in the
glossary on page 47. The glossary gives a brief
explanation of words that may be new to you.

Contents

What happened to the Russian Royal Family in 1918?

The 'executions' – the official version

The date, 17 July 1918. The place, Ekaterinburg in the Ural Mountains. The time, about 1.30am. Nicholas Romanov, his wife Alexandra Feodoronova and their five children, Alexei, Olga, Tatiana, Marie and Anastasia, were awakened and ordered to dress. Along with their five remaining servants and the family's pet spaniel, Jimmy, they were hurried to a basement room of the Ipatiev House (a house in Ekaterinburg owned by a man called Ipatiev) where they were being held captive. They believed that they were going to be moved to another place. But, as soon as they were all in the room, a squad of heavily armed men arrived. They told Nicholas that they had received orders to execute the family. Alexandra had only time to cross herself before the squad opened fire. Those who did not die in the hail of bullets were finished off with rifle butts and bayonets. Demidova, the maid, was pierced by thirty bayonet thrusts. She died clutching a pillow in which were hidden some of the priceless family jewels. Alexei, the 14-year-old heir to the throne, was kicked in the head and finally killed with two shots in his ear at close range. So perished Nicholas II, the last **Tsar** of Russia and all his family.

SOURCE 1

Tsar Nicholas II, his wife Alexandra, his son Alexei and four daughters, Olga, Marie, Tatiana and Anastasia. Taken in 1913.

'The World will never know what we did with them'

The bodies were quickly taken away from the house. They were carried in carts to a mine in the woods near Ekaterinburg called the 'Four Brothers'. Here they were hurriedly cut up, soaked in petrol and burnt. Sulphuric acid was poured on the charred remains to destroy the bones and so – it was hoped – remove the last traces of one of the richest and most powerful families in the world at that time.

The road to Ekaterinburg

Eighteen years earlier, at the dawn of the 20th century, the Tsar was the **absolute ruler** of the Russian people. To the majority he was their 'little father', loved and respected. But these years also brought increasing discontent and demands for change which finally erupted into revolution in February 1917 (see page 21). The Tsar was forced to **abdicate**.

A second revolution, in October 1917, brought to power the **Bolsheviks**, a group who were strongly opposed to the Tsar. A civil war followed between the armies of the Bolsheviks ('**Reds**') and those who still supported the Tsar ('**Whites**'). It was the fear that the White armies would free Nicholas that led to the order for the executions.

A 'history mystery'?

One week after the executions, the White armies captured Ekaterinburg. In January 1919, an investigation was begun under Judge Nicholas Sokolov (a White Russian). Besides the damaged room in the Ipatiev House, much of his evidence came from the Four Brothers Mine.

This included:

- fragments of precious stones and other jewels
- personal belongings of members of the family
- a finger alleged to belong to the **Tsarina**
- charred human bones. There were signs of these having been chopped and sawn up
- statements from the guards at the Ipatiev House.

Sokolov decided that the entire family had died. But other people at the time and since have claimed that the 'official' version may not be true. So the real fate of the Romanovs remains an intriguing mystery.

Russia showing the location of Ekaterinburg.

The evidence

SOURCE 2

The White armies – supporters of the Tsar – were closing in on Ekaterinburg, the main Red town in the Urals. We, the members of the Ural Soviet [Workers' Council], following the will of the people therefore decided that the ex-Tsar, Nicholas Romanov, should be shot. He has committed many bloody crimes against the people. The execution was carried out on the night of 16–17 July 1918. Romanov's family has been taken from Ekaterinburg to a place of greater safety.

The announcement of the Ural Soviet that Tsar Nicholas II had been shot. It was sent to Moscow and published there on 20 July 1918.

SOURCE 3

When I entered the room all the prisoners were lying on the ground, in various positions, in the midst of enormous pools of blood. All were dead, except for Alexei, who was still moaning. Before my eyes Yurovsky gave him two or three shots with his revolver and he stopped moaning. The sight of this massacre affected me so much that I felt sick and went out. . . I saw the following people dead: ex-Tsar Nicholas II, his wife Alexandra, his son Alexei, his four daughters, Dr Botkin, the cook, his assistant and maid.

Extract from the testimony of Judge Sokolov's star witness, Pavel Medvedev, a leader of the guard outside the Ipatiev House who claimed to be an eye-witness to the murder.

SOURCE 4

The 'murder room' in the Ipatiev House, Ekaterinburg. This was taken when Judge Sokolov was gathering evidence for his investigation.

Another version?

Sokolov's evidence seemed conclusive, but did he really examine all of the evidence? In 1976 Tom Mangold and Anthony Summers carried out an investigation for the BBC. They believed that Sokolov may well have been hasty in so readily closing the case. They posed some important questions:

Could the authorities be certain that all of the family was dead without having their bodies?

How reliable was Medvedev's testimony? It was given after he had surrendered, apparently voluntarily, to the White armies. Would he have given himself up in this way if he had really been involved in the Tsar's murder? He died mysteriously shortly afterwards. Either the Whites wanted to make the Bolsheviks look like cruel murderers or the Bolsheviks themselves wanted people to think that the Tsar was dead. This might have limited the opposition to them.

Some people have come forward who claim to be the surviving members of the Tsar's family (see box). Can all these 'pretenders' be dismissed as imposters?

The 'Pretenders'

1920s Italy: Marga Boodts claimed to be Olga.

1922 USA: Anna Anderson claimed to be Anastasia.

1926 North Africa: A young man claimed to be Alexei. He had haemophilia, a rare blood disorder. Alexei also had haemophilia.

1960 East Germany: Michal Goleniewski crossed the Berlin Wall to the West and was given US citizenship. He claimed to be Alexei.

SOURCE 5

She told them … that she was in fact the Grand Duchess Anastasia; that she had been present at the 'massacre' of the royal family and that she had been the sole survivor. She said she had hidden behind one of her sisters, had herself been hit by gunfire and had then lost consciousness. When she came to, she found herself with the family of a soldier who had rescued her at the last minute.

From the account of Anna Anderson, who claimed to be Anastasia in 1922. (Summers and Mangold, The File on the Tsar, 1976.)

SOURCE 6

Anna Anderson in Berlin, 1925.

SOURCE 7

As a result of my work on this case, I became convinced that the royal family was alive. It appeared to me that the Bolsheviks had shot someone in the room in order to simulate [fake] the murder.

From a report by Captain Malinovsky of the White Army, after a search of the Ipatiev House in July 1918.

SOURCE 8

On 17 July, a train with the blinds down left Ekaterinburg for an unknown destination and it is believed that the surviving members of the royal family were in it.

Sir Charles Eliot, British High Commissioner in Siberia, October 1918. Eliot was asked by the British government to find out what happened to the royal family.

SOURCE 9

On July 1 everything was ready and the plane took off. Success was not complete and I find it too dangerous to give details. One child was literally thrown into the plane at Ekaterinburg, much bruised, and brought to Britain, where she still is. But I am sure that if her identity were known she will be tracked down and murdered as the heir to the Russian throne.

Extract from the diary of Richard Meinertzhagen who, in 1918, was involved in an alleged plan by the British Secret Service to free Tatiana from captivity in Ekaterinburg.

SOURCE 10

I work as a conductor on the Omsk railway … After the Bolsheviks announced that they had shot the former Tsar Nicholas II . . .I asked Varakushev [a guard at the house] if was true. He told me that they were taken to Ekaterinburg station where they were pu in a railway carriage and sent off to Perm.

Evidence given by Alexander Samoilov, a railway official, in September 1918. Judge Sokolov dismissed this evidence.

SOURCE 11

The Bolsheviks removed almost all the Romanovs from Ekaterinburg alive … only the royal servants were killed at the Ipatiev House and it was their bodies that were disposed of at the mine.

The conclusions of Summers and Mangold, The File on the Tsar, 1976.

QUESTIONS

Now either individually or in groups:

1   **Work out the various theories for what happened to the Tsar and his family.**

2   **Consider the strengths and weaknesses of the evidence for each.**

3   **Which do you think is the most likely explanation?**

he end of the mystery?

....

or over 70 years, many people in the **USSR (Union of Soviet
ocialist Republics)** did not know anything of the fate of their
st Tsar. They assumed that he had simply abdicated and gone
to exile.

nce 1987, however, more information has become available.
he awful possibility that the whole family was brutally
urdered is now widely known. There is a need to find the truth
d to give the last remains of the royal family a proper burial.

1991, bones were found during a search of the woods near
katerinburg. They were brought to Britain to be tested by
rensic scientists to decide finally whether or not they are the
mains of the Tsar and his family. In July 1993, the scientists
ached their conclusions. Was the mystery solved?

DNA TESTS IDENTIFY TSAR'S SKELETON

British scientists have proved 'virtually beyond doubt' that bones unearthed in eastern Russia in 1991 are those of the murdered Tsar Nicholas II and his family. They conclude that there is a 98.5 per cent probability that the bones are the remains of the Romanovs.

Two members of the royal family remain unaccounted for: the Tsar's heir, Alexei, and one of his daughters.

*Extract from an article in **The Times**, 10 July 1993.*

OURCE *12*

*Photographs of Alexandra (left) and Tsar Nicholas II
(right), together with bones thought to be theirs.
From an article in **The Times**, 18 September 1992.*

SOURCE *14*

An end to the Anastasia Mystery? Maybe

A Russian government commission in Moscow say they have resolved one of the enduring mysteries of the 20th century. The commission reported on Tuesday that Princess Anastasia was indeed murdered along with her family by the Bolsheviks in 1918. If true, the report could bring to an end one of the most bizarre and intriguing quests of the century…

*Extract from the
**International Herald
Tribune**, New York,
7 September 1994.*

An end to the Anderson factor

In 1984, Anna Anderson died. In 1994 some of those who believed her claims to be Anastasia, paid for scientific tests to be carried out on some of her body tissue. This tissue had been removed during an operation before she died. They believed that Anna's claims would be proved right once and for all. The results were certainly conclusive.

SOURCE 15

DNA tests have disproved Anna Anderson's claims to be Anastasia. Science has triumphed where historians failed. Anna Anderson was an imposter. She was not Anastasia, the daughter of the last Tsar of Russia.

Extract from the **Sunday Times**, 9 October 1994.

THINK IT THROUGH

Study the new evidence carefully. Does this new evidence change the conclusions you have already reached?

SOURCE 16

Prince Philip's great-grandmother was also Anastasia's grandmother. Blood samples taken from Prince Philip did not match Anna Anderson's tissue in the DNA test. If Anna had been Anastasia the samples would have matched, because Anastasia was a blood relation of Prince Philip's.

ACTIVITY

What happened to the Russian Royal Family in 1918?

Now that you have studied all of the evidence available to date, the time has come for you to make up your own mind about what you think happened at Ekaterinburg in July 1918.

Look back over the work you have already completed. Try to explain your conclusions, using what you have learnt as well as the evidence. In your answer you should consider:

- the different theories
- the strengths and weaknesses of the evidence for each
- the extent to which we can be certain about what happened
- the questions that remain unanswered.

Was Nicholas II responsible for his own downfall?

How did Nicholas II come to such an apparently brutal end? The purpose of this part of the book is to explore the events and personalities in Russia to try and explain why there was a revolution in 1917. The Tsar, himself, is a good starting point.

Nicholas, the man

Nicholas was born in 1868. His accession to the throne was sudden and unexpected, for his father, Alexander III, was only 49-years-old when he died in November 1894.

He is portrayed by those who knew him as a charming, kind and deeply religious man. He enjoyed the countryside and the outdoor life. He had all the qualities of a fine human being. If he had been a **constitutional monarch** (a king with limited powers), like his cousin, King George V of Great Britain, he would probably have also been a good ruler. But Russia, at the beginning of the 20th century, was still an **absolute monarchy**. Historians seem to agree that Nicholas lacked the necessary qualities to rule a rapidly changing country.

Nicholas, the Tsar

There is no doubt that Nicholas loved his country and his people. However, as events will show, he did not understand the changes that were taking place in Russia. He also seems to have been unwilling to make the kind of decisions that might have prevented revolution. This involved sharing power with the people. But, this he refused to do, insisting that his power should be passed on unchanged to his son.

SOURCE 1

Nicholas II painted by Valentin Serov, a Russian artist who lived between 1865 and 1911.

SOURCE 2

The Emperor Nicholas II has a peculiar gift of charm. I do not know anyone who was not charmed by him the first time that they were presented to him. He charms both by simple kindness… and by his wonderful good feeling.

Sergei Witte, the Tsar's Prime Minister in 1905.

SOURCE 3

Let all know that in devoting all my strength on behalf of the welfare of my people, I shall defend the principles of autocracy [total power] as unswervingly as my dead father.

Nicholas II, on his accession to the throne, in 1894.

SOURCE 4

Wonderful, unforgettable day in my life, the day of my engagement to my darling, adorable Alix.

An extract from Nicholas's diary for April 1894.

Alexandra, Alexei and the haemophilia factor

In 1894, whilst still in mourning for his father, Nicholas married a German princess, Alix of Hesse. He adored her, but his devotion, unfortunately, was to have political consequences. Alexandra (as she became known in Russia) was very determined and interfered in the political decisions that Nicholas had to make. He followed her advice, but it was rarely sound. This made her unpopular.

They had five children. Four daughters were born between 1895 and 1901. Then, in 1904, Alix gave birth to a son and heir – Alexei. But their joy was short-lived. Within weeks of his birth it became clear that the child was suffering from haemophilia, a disorder of the blood. Any slight injury caused bleeding which could not be stopped. A knock caused intensely painful, internal bleeding.

The couple were devastated, especially Alexandra, who knew that she had passed this terrible disorder on to her son. In 1904, doctors knew very little about haemophilia or how to treat it. It seemed likely that the life of the **Tsarevich** would be short.

SOURCE 5

A private photograph, taken in 1905, of Nicholas with his baby son. The inscription reads: 'Nicky with his son'.

lexei's weakness was also a political roblem. Nicholas was afraid that if his nemies knew that his son was unlikely to ucceed him it would encourage them to nake even greater demands for change. The hild's illness had to be kept a secret at all osts. Alexei lived quietly at Tsarkoe Selo (the sar's village) outside St Petersburg. lexandra spent a great deal of time there rith him. People at the royal court in t Petersburg saw this as a snub. This also nade her unpopular.

Rasputin

rom 1905, the couple's anxiety for Alexei led hem to become dependant on a 'holy man', regory Rasputin. He was coarse, dirty and isgusting. But the hypnotic powers he ossessed appeared to heal Alexei. Alexandra ame to rely on him and called for him vhenever the child was ill. Rasputin took dvantage of the Tsarina's weakness to nfluence political decisions. Some people hought he was ruling Russia! He was nurdered by a group of noblemen in 1916. But, by this time, the reputations of Nicholas nd Alexandra had been badly damaged.

SOURCE 6

The illness of the Tsarevich cast its shadow over the whole of the concluding period of Tsar Nicholas II's reign and alone can explain it. Without appearing to be, it was one of the main causes of his fall, for it made the influence of Rasputin possible. This resulted in the fatal isolation of the sovereigns who lived in a world apart, wholly absorbed in a tragic anxiety which had to be concealed from all eyes.

Written after the death of the family by Pierre Gilliard, Alexei's tutor.

QUESTIONS

1　**List Nicholas's good and weak points.**

2　**In what ways did Alexei's illness harm the royal family?**

3　**Do you think that this was enough by itself to end the monarchy in Russia ?**

4　**What else would you like to know about Russia at this time? Make a list of questions.**

SOURCE 7

The body of the murdered Rasputin, 1916. He was poisoned, shot and finally drowned in the River Neva.

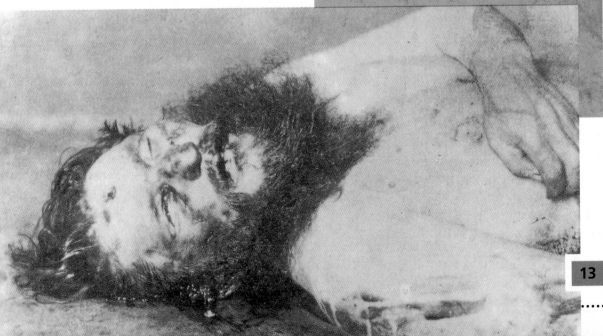

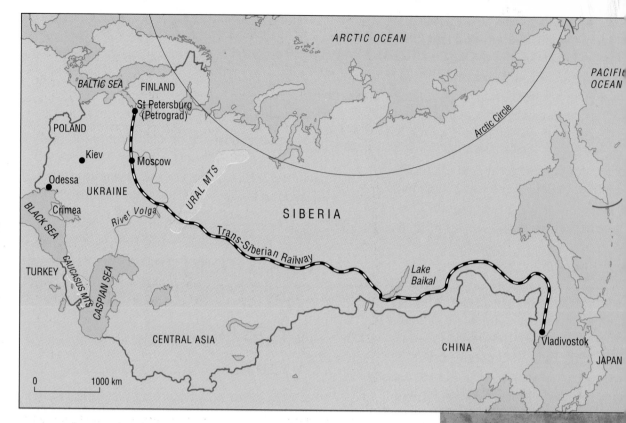

The Russian Empire in the reign of Nicholas II.

Did the Tsar have an impossible task?

Some historians think that Nicholas was doomed from the beginning, because of the many problems that faced him when he became Tsar.

The Tsar's Empire

Nicholas ruled a vast empire. It occupied one-sixth of the world's land surface. Its peoples were very different, for they included Ukrainians, Poles, Finns, Jews and Tartars. Only 40% were Russians. Their languages, customs and religions were very different. Many were restless, for they wanted independence and hated Russia. This made Nicholas's job even harder.

The situation was made worse because the population was growing very rapidly. Between 1815 and 1900 it had doubled, reaching 163 million by 1917. Of these, 80% were peasant farmers. The rise in population hit these people very hard. Their land had to be divided up so many times that it became a struggle to survive. So the peasants became restless and discontented.

SOURCE **8**

Before 1914 most Russians were peasants – people who farmed land they either owned or rented from a landlord. In Russia before 1914 farming methods were inefficient. In most villages the land was divided into three large fields. The peasants farmed strips in each field. One field was left uncultivated each year to regain its fertility. This was a waste of land.

*From **Russia and the USSR: 1905–1964**, by Alan White, 1994.*

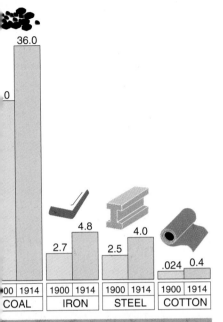

How Russian industry grew, 1900–14.

Russia had been left behind in the 19th century, as other countries became industrialized. But between 1891 and 1900, Russian industry began to grow. Around Moscow and St Petersburg, in Ukraine and Russia's Polish lands, men and women moved to towns, where they lived and worked in dreadful conditions. They were unprotected from hazards and openly exploited. Their discontent and anger often erupted into violent strikes.

Social inequalities

But the Tsar seemed to have little interest in these problems. From 1893, his Finance Minister, Sergei Witte, raised taxes to provide money for industry and for the building of the Trans-Siberian Railway. These taxes hit the workers and peasants the hardest. But the reforms that the workers demanded did not come. Instead, from 1902, demonstrations were put down ruthlessly by Plehve, the Tsar's Minister of the Interior. Workers and peasants soon began to listen carefully to talk of revolution.

Industrialization did not help to reduce the enormous gap that existed between the Tsar, the wealthy nobility, the powerful **Orthodox Church** and the mass of the people. Instead, it created a wealthy, educated, middle class made up of industrialists, lawyers, bankers and businessmen. Educated people pressed the Tsar for political power. From them came the leaders of the revolution.

OURCE *10*

Working conditions in the towns were often very bad. The wages were very low and the accident rate was very high. Living conditions for the industrial workers were as bad as those for the peasants in the countryside. Many lived in huge barracks attached to factories. Some families even lived in the factories.

From Russia 1917–1945, by Clare Baker, 1990.

QUESTIONS

1 Make a list of Nicholas's problems.

2 Draw two columns. In one write the problems that could have been solved and in the other suggest the methods he could have used.

3 From what you already know about Nicholas, why do you think that he did nothing?

4 Were any of his problems impossible to solve? Explain your answer.

Nicholas's restless inheritance

Nicholas's problems were not all of his own making. He had not inherited a peaceful realm. There had been unrest and violence throughout the 19th century in the cause of freedom and a better life. Until 1861, the mass of Russian peasants had been **serfs** (slaves) owned by their masters. In that year, Nicholas's grandfather, Alexander II, had given them their freedom. But life for the peasants became even worse afterwards. Alexander II was assassinated in 1881, because his reforms did not go far enough.

After the **emancipation** of the serfs, local councils called zemstva were set up. They were able to provide welfare and public services. They also gave some educated, middle-class Russians an opportunity to be involved in local government. By the end of the century these people from the middle class had formed groups opposed to the Tsar that wanted to be involved in government.

Nicholas's grandfather and father used their secret police, the **Okhrana**, to root out other dangerous revolutionaries. Many were imprisoned in Siberia or exiled. Nicholas II continued this policy of treating critics harshly, but it only increased opposition. This showed itself in acts of terrorism and murder.

Early in Nicholas's reign, revolutionaries were forming themselves into political parties. They were not all agreed on the solutions to Russia's problems. Some wanted parliamentary government. Others were influenced by the work of Karl Marx, a German, whose writings set out the idea of a working-class revolution in order to get a fairer system of government. These were the Bolsheviks. It was only a matter of time before such restless undercurrents would break out onto the surface. Meanwhile, the popularity of the Tsar continued to decline.

SOURCE 11

A Russian revolutionary cartoon of 1900, showing the social order. The workers are shown supporting the middle and upper classes. The royal family is at the top.

SOURCE 12

The Russian people are revolutionary by instinct.

Michael Bakunin (1814–1876), a Russian reformer famous for criticizing Tsarist rule.

SOURCE 13

Russia is a cauldron of boiling water, tightly closed and placed on a fire that is becoming hotter and hotter. I fear an explosion.

An observation made by a French traveller in St Petersburg, 1830.

he War with Japan, 904–1905

1904, Russia was one of the great wers. It had the largest army in the orld. Russians believed that it was e best. They were soon to be rribly disillusioned. In 1904, without urning, the Japanese attacked the ussian fleet in Port Arthur. After any years of rivalry between the two untries the time had come to settle ings finally.

he start of the war was greeted with thusiasm by the people. The Tsar's opularity rose dramatically. But poor mmunications prevented the rapid ovement of Russian troops and pplies. The result was disastrous. e great Russian army was defeated the Battle of Mukden and a second seige of rt Arthur resulted in a Russian surrender. The struction of the Russian fleet at Tsushima as the final catastrophe.

he effects of defeat at home were swift. The sar's popularity collapsed. His government was verely criticised by the middle classes. There ere huge workers' strikes, especially in St etersburg.

Bloody Sunday'

y the beginning of 1905, over 100,000 people St Petersburg were on strike, following sputes with their employers. In desperation, 9 January, a young priest, Father Gregory apon, organized a peaceful march to petition e Tsar for help (see box). The police were told oout the march and the route that it would take the Winter Palace. Families went along arrying pictures of the Tsar and singing hymns. ut, as they approached the palace, their way as blocked by mounted **Cossack** guards. nprovoked, they attacked the marchers. It as a massacre. At least 92 men, women and hildren were killed.

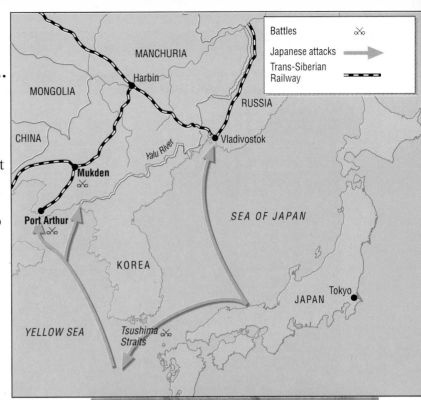

Map showing the battles of the Russo-Japanese War, 1904–1905.

Father Gapon's Petition

We ask for:

- a parliament elected by the people
- properly organized trade unions
- a minimum wage
- an eight-hour day
- education for the working classes

QUESTIONS

1   How useful are Sources 11–13 for finding out about Russia in the 1900s?

2   In what ways was the situation already hopeless by the time that Nicholas became Tsar?

*A painting from **Zhupel**, a Russian magazine, 1905. It shows the Tsar's soldiers charging the peaceful marchers on 9 January 1905 – 'Bloody Sunday'.*

SOURCE *15*

A cry of alarm rose as the Cossacks came down upon us. Our front ranks broke before them, opening to right and left, and down this lane the soldiers drove their horses, striking on both sides. I saw swords lifting and falling, the men, women and children dropping to the earth like logs of wood, while moans, curses and shouts filled the air.

Father Gapon, describing what happened on 'Bloody Sunday', 1905.

SOURCE *16*

'Bloody Sunday' destroyed the centuries old belief in the Tsar. This belief was shattered on 9 January 1905.

The view of Valeri Silenko, a history teacher in the Ukraine, 1994. Until 1991 the Ukraine was part of the USSR. It is now an independent country.

The 1905 Revolution

The Tsar was not at the Winter Palace. He was not told that the march was taking place. But, as far as the people were concerned, he was to blame for the terrible events of that day. The country erupted into violence and unrest. In towns all over the Empire the workers went on strike. In February 1905 the Tsar's uncle, Grand Duke Sergei was murdered; still the Tsar took no action. Workers' councils or **Soviets** were formed to organize the workers' action. Of these the largest was the St Petersburg Soviet. In June 1905, in the port of Odessa, the crew of the battleship, *Potemkin* mutinied. The loyalty of the army was also in question. In the countryside peasants attacked their landlords. The Tsar's government was on the point of collapse and the country was fast becoming out of control.

reform at last?

he time had come for the Tsar to act. He
as by now convinced of the seriousness of
e situation. In October 1905 he reluctantly
sued the October Manifesto. This was a
ocument in which the Tsar promised a
uma (an elected Parliament) that would
dvise him and his ministers. It would also
ave the power to make laws. This pleased
ome middle-class reformers but others
elieved Nicholas would not keep his word.
he strikes and riots continued throughout
005.

eter Stolypin

ergei Witte was made Prime Minister and
lections were held for the Duma. The Duma
rst met in May 1906. It soon became clear
at it had no real power. If Nicholas did not
ke what its members said, he dismissed
em. In June 1906, Peter Stolypin became
rime Minister. He managed to control the
tuation. He dealt harshly with the
evolutionaries, but at the same time began to
troduce land reforms in an attempt to make
fe easier for the peasants. In this way he
oped to make this large section of the
opulation loyal to the Tsar once more. But,
nfortunately for Nicholas, Stolypin was
ssassinated at the theatre in Kiev in 1911.
is work was incomplete.

QUESTIONS

1 Look at Source 14. Why do you think
   it was painted?

2 Look at Source 15. Do you think that
   the artist of Source 14 used this
   account of events by Gapon?

3 Could Nicholas have recovered his
   popularity in 1905? Use Source 16 and
   the diagram on this page to help you.

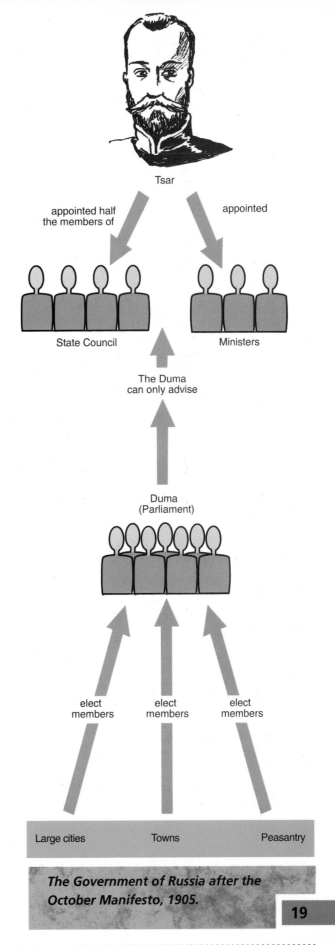

Tsar

appointed half
the members of

appointed

State Council

Ministers

The Duma
can only advise

Duma
(Parliament)

elect
members

elect
members

elect
members

Large cities   Towns   Peasantry

*The Government of Russia after the
October Manifesto, 1905.*

19

The First World War – the final catastrophe

The years between 1906 and 1914 were relatively peaceful. But in 1914, the fragile peace in Europe was shattered. Russia was a world power. On 1 August 1914, Germany declared war on Russia, and then on its ally France. Russia was now involved in the First World War.

Once again, there was an upsurge of patriotism and support for the Tsar as he and Alexandra saw the troops off to the Eastern Front. There had been improvements in the army since the Japanese war and hopes of a victory were high.

But, when the news from the front began to reach St Petersburg, it could not have been worse. Although the Russian armies had been successful at first, they were soon beaten by the Germans at the battles of Tannenburg and Masurian Lakes (1914). By 1915, there were claims that the army did not have enough arms, ammunition and equipment. By the summer of 1915, over one million men had been taken prisoner and 1,440,000 men killed. The army was being pushed back by the Gemans and the soldiers were sick with typhus and other diseases.

The heavy losses continued. In August 1915, the Tsar decided to go to the Front and take command of the armies himself, even though he was warned that it was very dangerous to leave St Petersburg. A renewed attacked by General Brusilov in 1916 was successful at first. But this was short lived. Russian losses remained high.

By the beginning of 1917 the number of soldiers deserting the army was on the increase.

In recent battles, one-third of the men had no rifles. These poor devils had to wait patiently until their comrades fell before their eyes and they could pick up weapons. The army is drowning in its own blood.

From a report by a Russian General at the Eastern Front, 1915.

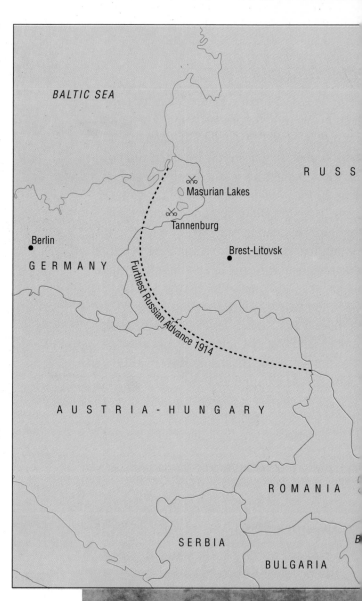

The Eastern Front in the First World War. The Russian army was defeated in 1914 at the battles of Tannenburg and Masurian Lakes.

Crisis at home

The First World War affected people at home very badly. There were serious food shortages, as there were no men to gather in the harvest. Prices rose beyond the reach of poorly-paid workers in the towns.

Alexandra and Rasputin

To make matters worse, Nicholas had left the government in the hands of his wife. This was unfortunate because she continued to be influenced by Rasputin until his death in 1916. Urged on by him, she called and dismissed a succession of elderly ministers who were incapable of dealing with the crisis.

The war also caused strong anti-German feeling. Alexandra was German! She had no idea how serious the situation had become by 1917. Isolated at the front, Nicholas followed all her advice.

Meanwhile, in St Petersburg, now renamed Petrograd, the soldiers, like the workers, were listening to revolutionary propaganda. They were driven to desperation by cold and hunger. Above all, they wanted an end to the war. In February, riots broke out in the streets as people queued for bread. The soldiers would not fire on the rioters. Russia was on the verge of revolution.

The February Revolution, 1917

The crisis caused by the First World War was directly responsible for this revolution. There had been hunger riots, strikes and demonstrations before. The crucial difference was that, in February 1917, young Russian soldiers in Petrograd gave up their loyalty to the Tsar and joined the people.

A Russian cartoon showing the power of Rasputin over the Tsar and Tsarina.

In February, the Duma complained to Nicholas about the way the war was being fought. He ignored these complaints and dismissed the assembly. This encouraged some members of the Duma to defy the Tsar and set up a **Provisional Government**, promising to introduce elections and a new constitution (set of laws about government) as soon as peace and order were restored. Without the support of the army, the Tsar had no choice but to abdicate.

A photograph of Russian soldiers taken in Petrograd in February 1917, after they had joined demonstrators. There are anti-Tsarist slogans on the banners they are carrying.

THINK IT THROUGH

How did the First World War lead to the February Revolution?

ACTIVITIES

Look at the following interpretation of Nicholas II's reign. It is the **Bolshevik** view of the Tsar, explained by Valeri Silenko, a history teacher in the former Soviet Union:

'The Tsar was portrayed as a person without will-power, who was incapable of ruling the country. He just sat on the throne and presided there. Nicholas was a person without a will. A nonentity.'

1   Go back over the work you have done already for this unit. Make a list of the evidence which supports the Bolshevik view of Nicholas.

2   Now make a list of the evidence that suggests that this view might be unfair.

3   Do you think that Nicholas brought about his own downfall? Use the evidence you have gathered to support your answer.

Was the October Revolution a victory for the Bolsheviks?

The overthrow of Tsarist rule caused great excitement. But what would replace it? How much support did the Provisional Government actually have? Would it succeed where the Tsar had failed?

The Provisional Government

The members of the Provisional Government were mostly middle class. They had no immediate ideas about how to run the country. Their policy was to wait until there was a properly elected assembly. This delay was a mistake because the peasants wanted land and the workers wanted better conditions. There was a general demand for an end to the war. But nothing was done to deal with any of these problems. The new government did, however, free political prisoners and allowed those who had been exiled by the Tsar to return to Russia.

The Petrograd Soviet

The position of the Provisional Government was weakened further because it had a rival – the Petrograd Soviet (Workers' Council). This came into being before the abdication of the Tsar. It was a council that represented the workers and soldiers in the city and was elected by them. Gradually, Soviets were set up in most of the towns and cities of Russia.

At first, the Soviet and the Provisional Government worked together. The 'deputies' (representatives) in the Soviet were quite moderate. Most of them belonged to the **Mensheviks**. This was a political group who wanted a socialist government (government by the people for the people) eventually, but realised that it might take time to achieve.

Their leader was Alexander Kerensky. He also became the leader of the Provisional Government in July 1917. However, the slow progress towards reform meant that impatient workers and soldiers turned more and more to the Soviet for action.

All might not have been lost if it had not been for the Bolsheviks. These were a more extreme group, who wanted a working-class revolution. They worked to weaken the Provisional Government by demanding peace immediately. At first they were a minority. However, in April 1917, they received a great boost to their cause. Their leader, Lenin, returned to Petrograd.

SOURCE 1

Alexander Kerensky, leader of the Petrograd Soviet and the Provisional Government, July 1917.

Vladimir Ilyich Lenin

Lenin had lived in exile since 1897, first in Siberia and then in Europe. He was a trained lawyer who had decided, as a young student, that the answer to Russia's problems lay in the work of the German writer and thinker, Karl Marx. The workers must rebel to destroy the old system and replace it with a government based on equality. Everything would be shared out fairly so that no-one had more than he or she needed. This became known as Communism.

There was little that Lenin could achieve in exile, so he had been excited by the revolution of 1905. He thought that his chance to return to Russia had come. But that opportunity passed.

However, Lenin learned two important lessons from the 1905 Revolution. Firstly, the need to be highly organized. Secondly, that the workers and peasants were a powerful force which he needed to have on his side if he were to succeed.

As soon as the news of the February Revolution reached Switzerland, where Lenin was living, he made plans to return to his homeland. He was helped by the Germans. They knew that Lenin would take Russia out of the First World War if he was successful.

'All power to the Soviets'

From the moment of his arrival at the Finland Station, Petrograd, Lenin began his attack on the Provisional Government. The Bolsheviks were a small party of about 24,000 members. By means of stirring speeches and the clever organization of his party workers, Lenin was able to influence the workers and soldiers in the Petrograd Soviet. The Bolsheviks came to dominate the Soviets in other towns and cities of Russia. The message was simple – if they wanted power and land they must take it!

SOURCE 2

Painting of the arrival of Lenin at the Finland Station, Petrograd, April 1917.

enin argued that it was
.e Soviets and not the
.rovisional Government
.at really represented
.e people because their
.presentatives were
.ected, unlike the
.rovisional Government.
.s the horrors of the war
.nd hardships at home
.ontinued, these ideas
.ecame very acceptable
. the workers, soldiers
.nd peasants.

The July Days

.ot that everything went
.asily for Lenin. There
.as still some support for
.erensky. Then, on 3–4
.uly, the workers,
.easants and soldiers
.ook to the streets once
.ore in Petrograd. They
.ooked for leadership
.om the Bolsheviks. But
.hey were not yet ready for revolution. The result was confusion.
.he party offices were smashed up; their newspaper, *Pravda*, was
.onfiscated. Lenin was forced to flee once more, this time to
.inland.

The Kornilov Affair

.hese events proved to be a temporary setback. Later, in August,
.erensky was faced with another problem. The Provisional
.overnment had appointed a new supreme commander of the
.rmy, General Kornilov. He was as critical of Kerensky and the
.Mensheviks as he was of Lenin and the Bolsheviks. His supporters
.vere landowners and businessmen. Many of them wanted to see
.he Tsar restored. Kornilov marched on Petrograd with the army.

.Kerensky was desperate for the support of the workers to defend
.Petrograd. He asked the Bolsheviks for help. The workers were
.rmed and trained ready to meet the enemy. They were organized
.nto a fighting force by another leading Bolshevik, Leon Trotsky.
.Kornilov's coup (takeover) was stopped. The workers believed that
.he Bolsheviks had saved them. Afterwards, they refused to give up
.heir arms. Kerensky was helpless.

SOURCE 3

Lenin speaking to the workers in May 1917. Trotsky is
standing below the platform on Lenin's left-hand side.

QUESTIONS

1 What were the
   differences
   between the
   Mensheviks and
   the Bolsheviks?

2 Make a list of the
   ways in which the
   Bolsheviks gained
   support from the
   workers.

3 Was the success of
   the Bolsheviks due
   to the failure of
   Kerensky and the
   Provisional
   Government?
   Explain your
   answer.

Trotsky and the Red Guard

In September 1917, Petrograd was still suffering from the effects of the war. Soldiers who were called up were refusing to fight. Food shortages remained serious. In these circumstances, the Bolsheviks gained even more support with their slogan: 'Peace, Bread and Land'.

In early October, Trotsky became the leader of the Petrograd Soviet. He began to train the Petrograd workers to overthrow the Provisional Government. These became known as the Red Guard. Also in October, Lenin returned to Petrograd in disguise. The time for a second revolution had arrived.

SOURCE 4

At night the street lights were few; in private houses the electricity was turned off from six o' clock until midnight. Robberies and house-breaking increased. In apartments men took turn at all night guard duty, armed with loaded rifles. This was under the Provisional Government.

Food was becoming scarce. The daily allowance of bread fell. There were times when no bread at all was available. For milk, bread, sugar and tobacco one had to queue long hours in the cold rain. I heard people in the breadlines saying how unhappy they were.

Of course, life for the rich went on much the same. The theatres were going every night, including Sundays.

*From **Ten Days that Shook the World** a book by John Reed, an American journalist, who was in Petrograd in 1917. Here Reed is describing life in Petrograd just before the October Revolution.*

SOURCE 5

The Women's Battalion that defended the Winter Palace in October 1917.

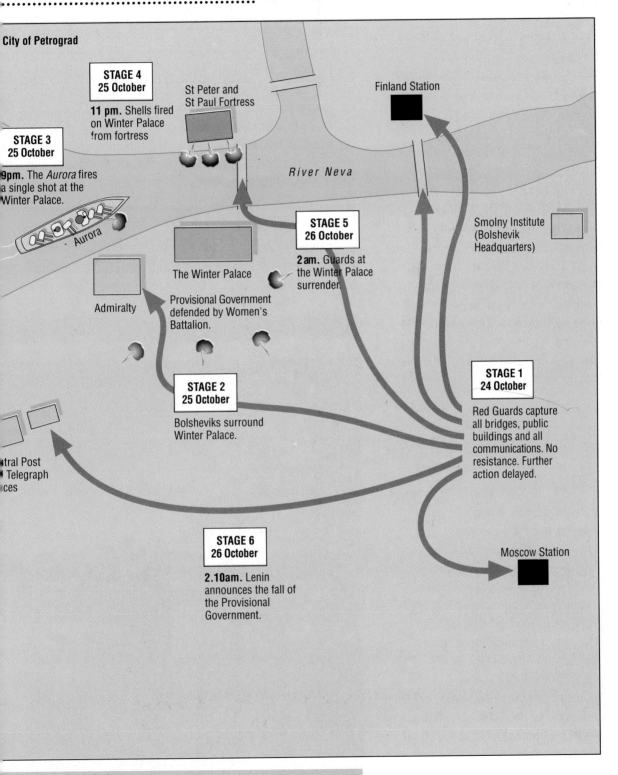

City of Petrograd

STAGE 4
25 October

11 pm. Shells fired on Winter Palace from fortress

St Peter and St Paul Fortress

Finland Station

STAGE 3
25 October

9pm. The *Aurora* fires a single shot at the Winter Palace.

River Neva

Aurora

STAGE 5
26 October

2 am. Guards at the Winter Palace surrender.

Smolny Institute (Bolshevik Headquarters)

The Winter Palace

Admiralty

Provisional Government defended by Women's Battalion.

STAGE 1
24 October

Red Guards capture all bridges, public buildings and all communications. No resistance. Further action delayed.

STAGE 2
25 October

Bolsheviks surround Winter Palace.

tral Post Telegraph ces

STAGE 6
26 October

2.10am. Lenin announces the fall of the Provisional Government.

Moscow Station

QUESTION

Jse Source 4 and the information on the map above to write a newspaper article describing the events in etrograd during October 1917.

On the morning of the 26 October, Lenin announced the end of the Provisional Government and the beginning of Soviet Government i.e. government by the people. But could Lenin keep his promise 'Peace, Bread and Land'? He had, at this point, only taken Petrograd. There were still many more millions of people who had either not heard of the Bolsheviks or did not know what they intended to do in Russia. The next three years were to plunge the Russian people into even greater pain and hardship than the darkest days of the First World War.

Peace and Bread

The Bolsheviks' immediate answer to the problem of bread was to encourage peasants to take food from the kulaks (richer peasants). This caused violence in the countryside.

In March 1918, a peace treaty was signed with Germany, the Treaty of Brest-Litovsk. This was welcomed by all the people, but it was a disaster for Russia. It gave Germany some of its most valuable land and industry. The rich grain lands of Ukraine, for example, and some of Russia's most prosperous industrial areas in the Baltic and Poland. This was a high price to pay for a country that was still suffering from the hardships of the war.

SOURCE 6

TO THE CITIZENS OF RUSSIA. The Provisional Governme is overthrown. State power has passed into the hands c the... Petrograd Soviet of Workers' and Soldiers' Deputie ... The cause for which the people were fighting... a democratic peace, the abolition of landlord property rights over the land, labour control over production, creation of a Soviet Government – that cause is securely achieved. LONG LIVE THE REVOLUTION OF WORKMEN SOLDIERS AND PEASANTS.

Extract from the notices that appeared on the streets of Petrograd on the morning of 26 October, after the Bolsheviks had seized the capital.

SOURCE 7

Lenin declaring Soviet power. Painted after the Revolution by Vladimir Serov, a Russian artist, who lived between 1910 and 1968.

he Civil War, 918–1921

enin and the Bolsheviks soon und out that there was strong pposition to their new overnment. People opposed e Bolsheviks for different easons:

- some still supported the Tsar
- some still supported the Provisional Government
- some wanted to be free from Russia altogether (e.g. the Poles, Ukrainians and Cossacks)
- some were totally opposed to the ideas of the Bolsheviks.

hese different groups joined orces which attacked Russia. hey were led by three men:

- Kolchak, who attacked from the east
- Yudenitch, who attacked from the west
- Denikin, who attacked from the south.

heir armies were known as he 'Whites'. The Bolshevik rmies were known as 'Reds'. A group of Czech soldiers who vere being transported across Russia at the time of the October Revolution also joined he 'Whites'. It was when these nen got dangerously close to Ekaterinburg in July 1918, that he order to execute the Tsar vas given. Forces from Britain and France landed at Archangel and supported the 'Whites' in a half-hearted way.

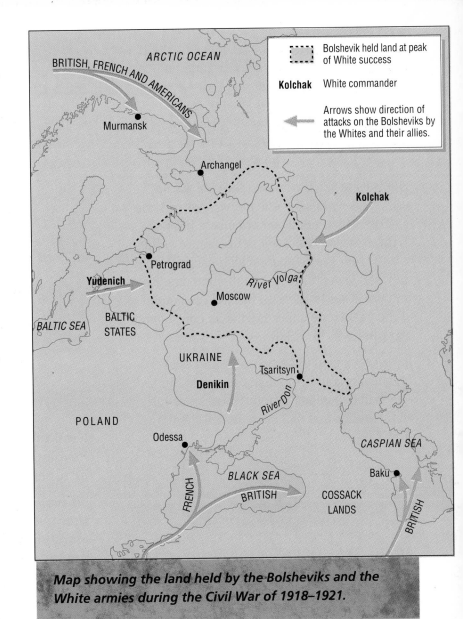

Map showing the land held by the Bolsheviks and the White armies during the Civil War of 1918–1921.

QUESTIONS

1 Why do you think that these notices (Source 6) appeared in the streets at that time?

2 Look at Source 7. Is this is an accurate picture of this event? Explain your answer.

3 'The Bolsheviks had successfully achieved power, but the Revolution had only just begun.' These words were written by a modern historian. Do you agree? Explain your answer.

After the Civil War

The civil war brought cruelty, hunger and disease to the Russian peasants whose villages were caught up in the fighting. The horrors and atrocities that took place were recorded in the works of Russian writers such as Boris Pasternak, who wrote *Dr Zhivago*.

The Bolsheviks finally won the civil war in 1921. This was partly due to the work of Leon Trotsky who trained and organized the Red Army. It was also a result of the failure of the White armies to co-operate with each other. If they had joined forces, then the outcome may have been very different. Instead the empire of the Tsar came under Bolshevik control and was renamed the USSR.

It now remained to be seen whether the Bolsheviks could complete the revolution they had begun and give the Russian people all the things that had been denied them by the Tsar.

SOURCE 8

The workers of the towns and some of the villages choke in the throes of hunger. The railroads barely crawl. The houses are crumbling. The towns are full of refuse. Epidemics spread and death strikes to the right and to the left. Industry is ruined.

Extract from a report in Pravda, the Bolshevik newspaper, 26 February 1920.

SOURCE 9

The lieutenant with beautiful womanish eye ... ran with his hands clutching his head. A bullet sent him jumping high as though ove a barrier. He fell and did not rise again. Two Cossacks cut down the tall captain. He caught at the blade of one sword and the blood poured out of his hand over his sleeve. He screamed like a child... The flying blades played over his face, but still he shrieked in a voice thin with pain and horro

An extract from Dr Zhivago, a novel, written by Boris Pasternak in 1957. Pasternak was opposed to the Bolsheviks.

ACTIVITY

Read this interpretation of the October Revolution written by a modern historian in 1993:

'It would be ... incorrect to consider that the Bolsheviks' planning for revolution was efficient, co-ordinated or properly thought out. It succeeded by default (failure of others) and accident rather than design.'

Do you think that this is true or was the October Revolution a complete victory for the Bolsheviks? Look back over your work. In your answer, think about what happened before, during and after October 1917.

How important was Lenin to the Russian Revolution?

Problems of evidence

There is nothing particularly special about the statue of Lenin (Source 1) except, perhaps, that it is still standing! Until recently, every town and city in the former Soviet Union had a similar statue at its centre because Lenin was regarded as the 'father of the USSR'. Often he is shown pointing the way forward, for Lenin was the hero of the Russian Revolution. He was regarded as the saviour of the people; the only man who had all the answers to Russia's problems, and knew the way forward. For all these reasons, he was greatly loved and respected by the people.

In 1991, however, the Soviet Union was broken up into independent states. The Communist Party (the Bolsheviks) lost its power. Now, the documents and other sources of evidence in the archives are slowly beginning to be explored. Suddenly, the Russian people have begun to get a different picture of Lenin and they do not like it. Many of the grand statues have been pulled down.

In this unit, it is important to appreciate that our view of Lenin may well have to change as more evidence becomes available in Russia.

SOURCE 1

Statue of Lenin in the centre of the regional town of Cherkassy, Ukraine, 1994.

It remains to be seen what future historians will make of the reputation of Lenin.

Who was Lenin and what were his origins?

Lenin's real name was Vladimir Ilyich Ulyanov. He was born in 1870 in Simbirsk, a town on the River Volga. His father was a school inspector and the family were quite comfortably off. Vladimir was a very intelligent and hard-working pupil. He was devoted to his elder brother, Alexander, who was executed in 1887 for his part in a plot to assassinate Tsar Alexander III. Many historians suggest that this was a very significant event in Lenin's life. From that moment, they claim, he hated the Tsar and devoted his energy and intelligence to creating a different kind of government for Russia. This is not to say, of course, that revenge was his only motive.

Lenin, the student rebel

As a student at the University of Kazan, he joined groups opposed to the Tsar. He was even expelled from the university for his political activities and for being involved in demonstrations. However, in 1892, he completed his education and became a lawyer.

During this period, he studied the writings of Karl Marx. Here he found what he thought were the answers to the problems that needed to be solved in Russia.

SOURCE 2

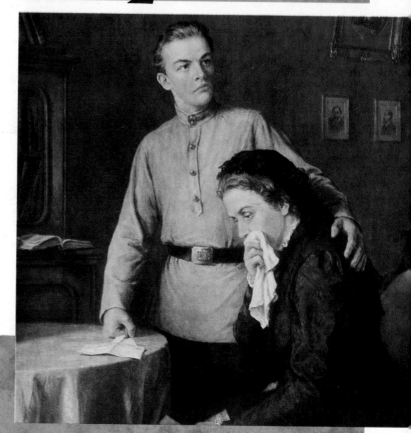

A well-known painting in Russia by Vladimir Serov. It shows the young Lenin, comforting his mother after the execution of his brother, Alexander. The picture is called, 'We must find another way'.

SOURCE 3

A short, stocky figure, with a big head set down on his shoulders, bald and bulging. Little eyes, a snubbish nose, wide, generous mouth and heavy chin; clean-shaven now but beginning to bristle with the well-known beard. Dressed in shabby clothes, his trousers much too long for him. Unimpressive, to be the idol of a mob, loved and worshipped as perhaps few leaders in history have been.

A description of Lenin from **Ten Days that Shook the World** by John Reed, an American journalist, who saw the events of 1917 in Petrograd.

What did Lenin learn from Karl Marx?

Marx (1818–1883) was a German who lived for some time in Britain. There he saw the effects of industrialization on the working people. He believed that they were used to create wealth for their middle-class bosses (capitalists). He argued that the workers should receive a fair share of the wealth that they were creating.

Marx knew that this would not happen unless the working classes rose up against their bosses and took what he regarded as rightfully theirs. The result would be a society where everyone would have a fair share of everything, according to their needs. Everyone would be equal; there would be no more social classes. This is what was meant by communism.

But how could a fairer society be achieved? The only way was to have a government that would represent the workers and protect their interests. Marx believed that this would happen in stages. Lenin took these ideas and adapted them to the situation in Russia. (Look carefully at the diagram).

Years in exile

For many years, Lenin was powerless to do anything for Russia. His criticisms of the Tsar resulted in imprisonment in 1895 and exile to Siberia in 1897. In 1900, he was allowed to leave Russia and began seventeen years of exile in western Europe. During this time, he joined a group of other Russian exiles who had been attracted to the ideas of Marx. They were called the 'Social Democrats'. Lenin's plans for a revolution in Russia made him stand out from the others in the group. But, what could he do in exile? He could only write letters, plan his revolution on paper and hope that his chance would come.

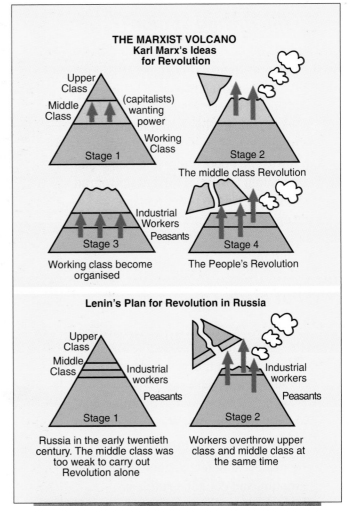

Diagram to show how Marx's theory could work. Lenin adapted this theory to fit Russia.

QUESTIONS

1 Look at Sources 1 and 3. Do both sources give you the same image of Lenin?
   Which do you think is more reliable?

2 Look at Source 2.
   How does this source help you to understand the motives for Lenin's future actions?

'To the Finland Station'

When Lenin had almost given up hope, his moment came in February 1917. The Tsar had been overthrown but the Provisional Government did not seem to have any policies that would improve the life of the people, and the war dragged on. It was the opportunity that Lenin had been waiting for. His return to Petrograd in April 1917 was to prove a major turning point in events in Russia, as Lenin seized the leadership of the Revolution.

What made Lenin a great leader?

At the time of his return, Lenin was not just the man with the 'right' ideas; he was also the man with the 'right' personality. What were the qualities that enabled him to become the leader of Russia?

- he had great determination, he lacked emotion and could be ruthless.
- he insisted on the complete loyalty of members of the Bolshevik Party.
- he recognized the importance of the party being highly organized and united.
- he had a clear view of what he wanted. He did not let anyone stand in his way. He stuck to his beliefs because he believed that he was right.
- he persuaded people by his stirring speeches, his writings and his newspaper articles.
- he spoke and wrote in a way that everyone could understand. He promised peace, bread, land and power to the workers, soldiers and peasants.

All of these characteristics can be seen in the events that followed his return. The Germans certainly thought that his presence in Petrograd would be dramatic or they would not have helped him to return.

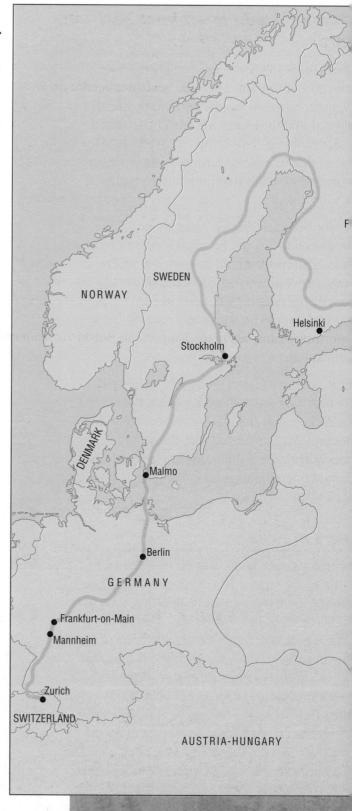

The route taken by Lenin when he returned to Russia in April 1917, with help from the Germans.

id Lenin's return make the October evolution inevitable?

n 3 April 1917 Lenin arrived at the Finland Station in etrograd. From this moment Lenin demanded the overthrow the Provisional Government. This did not mean, however, at it would happen automatically. His ideas (Source 5) were cepted by the ordinary people, who heard him speak, but t by all members of the Bolshevik Party. Some thought that e was right. Others did not accept him as their leader and ere shocked by his sudden and unexpected demands for a cond revolution. But this did not worry Lenin.

lso, in July 1917, Lenin was forced to flee again into exile in inland following the refusal of the Bolsheviks to lead a orking-class revolt at that time. It seemed that their days ere over. Yet Lenin kept up the enthusiasm of the party by is confident letters and newspaper articles. So, when the pportunity came again in October, the Bolshevik leadership as ready.

SOURCE 4

hotograph of Lenin in disguise, taken in uly 1917, when he fled to Finland.

SOURCE 5

Some of Lenin's plans for the Bolsheviks and Russia, which he announced on 4 April 1917:

1 Bolsheviks must oppose the war.
2 Power must pass from the middle classes to the working classes.
3 Bolsheviks must not support the Provisional Government.
4 The new government must be based on the Soviets of Workers' Deputies.
5 All landed estates must be taken away from their owners.

These plans were known as the 'April Theses'.

QUESTIONS

1 **Which of Lenin's personal qualities do you think were the most important in making him a successful leader?**

2 **Make a list of the points so far that suggest that Lenin was very important to the October Revolution.**

3 **Look back at the painting of Lenin at the Finland Station on page 24. Now look at Source 4. Which is more reliable? Explain your answer.**

Leon Trotsky

Lenin's achievement was not entirely of his own making. He also received great support from other Bolsheviks. Of these, the most outstanding was Leon Trotsky. He promised his support to Lenin in May 1917.

The part played by Trotsky must not be underestimated. He worked hard to get the army in Petrograd to support Lenin's plans. But his greatest contribution to the Revolution was the organization and training of the Red Guards. Without this, the October Revolution could not have taken place.

During the Civil War (1918–1921) he tirelessly toured round the Red Army, encouraging soldiers to fight on and not to give up.

Joseph Stalin

Joseph Stalin came from a peasant family in Georgia. He, too, was attracted by Marxist ideas and was sent into exile as a result. He was Lenin's idea of a 'good' Bolshevik. He was totally devoted to the party. He even robbed banks to swell the party funds! Above all, he supported Lenin and firmly believed that his plans for Russia were the right ones. He worked hard in the local workers' soviets (councils) to get them to support Lenin.

Some historians think that, in the course of time, either of these men – and others as well – were capable of leading a second revolution. But Lenin clearly provided the inspiration in October 1917. He decided the time of the revolution, even though he stood back whilst others carried it out.

SOURCE 6

A photograph of Trotsky, taken in 1917.

SOURCE 7

Gomel was just about to fall into the enemies hands when Trotsky arrived. Then everything changed and the tide began to turn.... He made a speech. We were lifted by the energy which he carried wherever a critical situation arose.

A Red Army officer describes the effect of a visit by Trotsky to the front lines during the Civil War of 1918–1921.

Stalin, as pictured in the files of the Okhrana, the Tsar's secret police, 1912–13. Stalin was imprisoned several times for robbing banks.

Did Lenin have the answers?

Once Lenin had power it remained to be seen whether he could keep the promises he had made. After all, neither Lenin nor the leading Bolsheviks had any experience of government. They had also spent much of their adult lives away from Russia.

Peace: Lenin immediately took steps to keep his first promise. Negotiations began with the Germans to end the war for Russia. He believed that this could be achieved with very little cost to Russia. He was terribly wrong. The Treaty of Brest-Litovsk, signed in 1918, robbed Russia of its grainlands and much of its oil (see page 28).

Government: Lenin kept his promise to hold elections for a Constituent Assembly (a body that would truly represent the people). But the Bolsheviks did not have enough seats to be the majority party. Lenin, therefore, had to act quickly to make sure that the party stayed in power.

The new assembly met only once. The Bolsheviks claimed that power should be in the hands of the Soviets. A Congress of Soviets replaced the Constituent Assembly. It was made up of representatives from all the local Soviets where Bolshevik support was strong. But the real base of power was a small committee of Bolsheviks called the Council of People's **Commissars**. They changed their name to the Communist Party. Lenin was the leader. Trotsky was Commissar for Foreign Affairs. Stalin was Commissar for Nationalities.

No other parties were allowed. Critics were dealt with by the Cheka, the Bolsheviks' secret police force. In 1923 Russia became the Union of Soviet Socialist Republics (USSR) and Moscow replaced Petrograd as the capital.

Land and Bread: After the October Revolution, Lenin allowed the land to be divided amongst the peasants because he needed their support. But he knew that they could not have complete freedom. The towns and cities were still starving. In 1917, the peasants were hoarding food because, during the war, the workers were not producing goods that could be exchanged for food.

During the Civil War (1918–1921), Lenin had to take strong measures to get food to the towns and cities. Peasants were made to grow more and to give their crops to the government. If they resisted, they were punished. This policy was called War Communism. In spite of this, food production continued to fall. Then drought in the summer of 1921 led to famine. About five million people died of hunger and disease – more than in the First World War and the Civil War. These were desperate times for Lenin and the Communists. Their harsh policies made these natural disasters harder for the people to bear. People who had previously supported the Bolsheviks began to have second thoughts. Where was the freedom that Lenin had promised? Lenin had to find another way if he was to stay in power.

Lenin's New Economic Policy

Lenin realised that, for the time being at least, he was unable to destroy **capitalism** completely, because the economy of the country was so weak. Even though the government had taken over the banks it di[d] not have enough money to help industry to grow. In March 1921 Lenin introduced his Nev[w] Economic Policy (NEP). This allowed a certai[n] amount of private trade, especially by the wealthier peasants (kulaks). The people had t[o] be fed, or they could not work and the country would never get on its feet again. A certain percentage of the crop was taken by the government at a low price. The peasants were then free to sell the rest at their own price.

A similar system operated in industry, where factory owners were allowed to run their factories and to make some profit. By 1924, there had been some improvement in the supply of food.

SOURCE 9

Delegates from the Villages visiting Lenin.
Painted by Vladimir Serov in 1950.

The death of Lenin

Lenin's New Economic Policy shocked his Bolshevik comrades, including Trotsky. They believed that he had abandoned his Marxist principles. But Lenin believed that there would have to be a gradual change and, in the meantime, some form of capitalism controlled by the government was necessary. How long would it last? This question cannot be answered because Lenin died before the full effects of his policies could be seen.

In 1918, Lenin had been shot by a young woman called Fanya Kaplan. He recovered, but four years later, he had a stroke, which left him partially paralysed and weak. He died in January 1924, following a further stroke. His body was embalmed and placed in a special tomb outside the **Kremlin** for all to see. It remained there until the break up of the Soviet Union in 1991.

Lenin had lived a very simple life and hated fuss. His final resting place was an indication of the great admiration of the Russian people, who paid their respects to him in thousands after his death.

He remained a great hero until the dramatic changes of 1991. The Russian people have now become very critical of Lenin. Worst of all has been the recognition that it was probably Lenin himself who ordered the execution of the Tsar and his family at Ekaterinburg in July 1918.

QUESTIONS

1   Make a list of the evidence from these pages that supports Source 10.

2   Make a list of the evidence that supports Source 11.

3   Do you agree with the views of Lenin expressed in Sources 10 and 11?

4   Look at Source 9. What impression does it give you of Lenin and the peasants? Is your impression supported by the facts in this section?

SOURCE 10

When I was at school we were taught that Lenin was the greatest ideologist [thinker], the greatest and the wisest man in the whole world because of what he did for Russia.

Vasilya Ananiev, a student in the former Soviet Union, speaking about Lenin in 1994.

SOURCE 11

Lenin did not seize power. It just dropped into his lap. The fate of Russia was decided by the history of the early 20th century, not by Lenin. If it had not been him there would have been someone else.

Valeri Silenko, a history teacher in the Ukraine (part of the former Soviet Union), speaking in 1994.

ACTIVITY

How important was Lenin to the Russian Revolution?

Look back over this unit and the tasks that you have already completed. In making up your mind, you should consider :

- **Lenin's personality and beliefs.**

- **How the situation in Russia helped Lenin.**

- **The support that Lenin got from other leading Bolsheviks.**

- **Lenin's policies after the Revolution.**

- **Your views as to what might have happened in Russia without Lenin's influence.**

What did the Revolution achieve?

The purpose of this unit is to consider the effects on the Russian people of the 1917 Revolution. This is difficult, because for so long there has been a strong fear of the USSR and Communism. So people in the West are reluctant to suggest that anything good came from the Revolution. It is important, however, to try to see its effects through Russian eyes for, until recently, the Revolution was regarded with pride. It was a great moment in Russian history.

SOURCE 1

After the Revolution a new life began for us. We got rid of the bourgeoisie [middle classes] and won our freedom! … . It was difficult to believe that until quite recently land-owners had driven about in the town in elegant carriages and moustachioed policemen with sabres had patrolled the streets. The owner of the factory had been an Englishman, Hughes, and his workers toiled in the flames as if they were in hell. But we had put an end to exploitation for ever . . . the hated words 'Your Honour', 'Master' were no longer to be heard. Armed workers patrolled the streets and addressed each other as comrade. Comrade! What a marvellous word it was, full of warmth and happiness… . I had got to love it and repeated it hundreds of times a day.

*This is an extract from a short story, **Red Flags over the Town** by Leonid Kharikov. It is in a children's story book, **The Winds of October**. The authors of all the stories were teenagers in 1917 and lived through the Revolution. It has been translated from the Russian.*

SOURCE 2

ВЕЛИКОМУ ЖОВТНЮ
СЛАВА !

An example of a greetings card sent each year in the former Soviet Union to celebrate the October Revolution. The message on the front says, 'Glory to Great October'.

SOURCE 3

A special set of stamps to commemorate the 60th anniversary of the October Revolution.

id the quality of life of the eople improve?

ter the October Revolution, Lenin troduced a number of reforms which were tended to improve the life of the Russian eople:

- he attempted to distribute wealth more fairly by reducing large salaries. The rich were encouraged to 'lend' money
- he gave women equal rights
- he tried to improve the quality of life by making education available to peasants and workers
- he provided education for youngsters as he recognised that they were the country's future.

y the time of his death, enin's New Economic olicy was bringing some nprovement, especially in ie supply of food. The easants were also given ome rights over ownership f land.

ut it was to take some time r the effects of these eforms to really benefit the eople. The Revolution rought the horrors of the ivil War. The famine of 921–2 also had devastating ffects on the people.

Trudging on foot, loaded with sacks, bundles and babies, exhausted young mothers who had lost their milk, driven out of their minds by the horrors… abandoned their children… . A quick death, they said, was better than a slow death by starvation.

*Extract from **Dr Zhivago** by Boris Pasternak, 1957.*

SOURCE 5

Victims of the Russian famine, 1921.

SOURCE 6

he Bolsheviks are making great efforts for the schools. The utmost s done for children from four to eight… .These children get the best foods … .They get good clothing and free shoes and aundry… . The children come to school with collars of lice around heir necks. … . The scarcity of soap makes it impossible for parents o wash the children or the children's clothes.

*From **Memoirs of a Revolutionary** by Victor Serge, 1963.*

Did the people gain more freedom and power?

Lenin had promised: 'All power to the Soviets'. But it soon became clear that the real power was in the Kremlin, in Moscow, where Lenin was dominant. The democratic government that he had promised never materialized. Lenin's secret police, the Cheka, were not very different from the Tsar's Okhrana in silencing criticism.

The harshness of the Bolsheviks' treatment of the workers and peasants led many to feel that they had exchanged one **tyranny**, that of the Tsar, for another. In 1921, the sailors of Kronstadt naval base mutinied in protest. They had supported the Bolsheviks but were now disillusioned by their harsh policies and cruel methods. Their actions spoke for thousands of others, but it got them nowhere. They were simply shot.

Those parts of the former Russian Empire that had wanted independence at the time of the Tsar were no better off. The attempt by Ukraine, for example, to take freedom, was quickly put down. On the other hand, by the time of Lenin's death, the USSR was being governed more efficiently than at the time of the Tsar.

The USSR and the West

The Communist Government in Russia caused great concern in the democratic countries of western Europe. Marx said that the working-class revolution should be international. Lenin also believed in this. He encouraged Communists in other countries – for example, Germany and Hungary. So governments of countries such as Britain, France and the USA became nervous and suspicious of the changes in Russia. This seriously weakened Russia's relations with the World powers.

QUESTIONS

1　According to Source 1, how did the Revolution help the people?

2　Look at Sources 2 and 3. How do they help us to understand the importance of the Revolution to the Russian people?

3　Does Source 6 prove that there were real improvements after the Revolution? Explain your answer.

The Stalin Years

Lenin was succeeded by Joseph Stalin, who was determined to complete the communist revolution. This meant that everything would be owned and controlled by the State. Above all, Russia's industries had to grow. The USSR had to become **self-sufficient** because Stalin did not want to trade with capitalist countries. Between 1924 and 1953 Stalin modernized the USSR. In addition to developing industry, he ensured that the people were better housed and the children better educated than before the Revolution.

SOURCE 7

Industrial Growth, 1927– 1937

	1927–8	1932	1937
Coal	35.4	64.3	128.0
Oil	11.7	21.4	28.5
Pig-iron	3.3	6.2	14.5
Steel	4.0	5.9	17.7

(million tonnes)

Production in the heavy industries increased under Stalin.

VE YEAR PLANS

ch industry was set a production target by the government, ich had to be reached in five years. Biggest targets were set heavy industries like coal-mining, steel and engineering. orkers were set targets and rewarded for high output g. holidays.

COLLECTIVE FARMS

Peasants' land was joined together to make large collective farms. Modern machinery and tools were shared between the farmers. The Kulaks (rich peasants) were against this change. They were sent to labour camps by Stalin. It is believed that three million Kulaks died in these camps in the 1930s.

HOW STALIN MADE THE USSR
A COMMUNIST COUNTRY

1927-53

ROPAGANDA

alin used posters, paintings and otographs to make people believe was doing good for the country.

EDUCATION

Good education was important for the country. Children were also brought up to respect Lenin and believe in Communism.

HOUSING

Blocks of small apartments were built, with space allocated according to size of family. There was a shortage of consumer goods. People were certain of essentials but there were no luxuries.

ut success was achieved at a terrible price. Forced labour nd concentration camps were set up to deal with **dissidents**. illions of people were murdered or disappeared without . ace especially during the **purges** of 1934–1938. Censorship f literature, State radio and control of the media kept the ajority of the people in ignorance. They had no contact with e world outside. Stalin acted as a dictator, but to many ussians, he was a popular and much loved leader – another ero of the Revolution that the people regarded as the reatest event in their history.

ACTIVITY

What did the Revolution achieve?

Look back carefully over the information in this ection. What are your conclusions? Think about:

- How much the USSR had changed by 1937.

- What people had wanted before the Revolution and what they actually got as a result.

- What the people in the USSR thought about the Revolution and why.

SOURCE *8*

Agricultural Output, 1928–1933

	1928	1930	1933
Grain (million tonnes)	73.3	83.5	68.4
Cattle	70.5	52.5	38.4
Pigs	26.0	13.6	12.1
Sheep and Goats	146.7	108.8	50.2

(in millions)

The decline in farming was due to the peasants' reaction to collective farming and to the increasing amounts of grain demanded by the government. They protested by growing less.

When the Curtain opened and tl Wall came down

SOURCE *1*

Extract from **The Independent**, Friday 10 November 1989.

BERLIN WALL BREAKS OPEN: EAST GERMANS START TO TRAVEL FREELY AS 28 YEAR OLD BARRIER FALLS

This is the best news the German people have heard since 1945. But it's right to look back: at the huge, artfully built frontiers of wire and lights, towers and minefields, dogs tethered to wires, sensor devices and mantrap guns, sanded death-traps, helmeted men with guns.

There, on the border of the Berlin Wall, hundreds of human beings died and hundreds were horribly maimed. The dogs howled and raved in the night. Sometimes there would be explosions, and then the screaming which might be human or might be a roe deer blown in half by a mine. This is what is over now.

The opening of the Berlin Wall and its subsequent destruction have been key events in the last decade of the 20th century. Equally important was the opening of the invisible barrier across Europe that Winston Churchill described in 1946, as an 'Iron Curtain'. After the Second World War, the Iron Curtain and Berlin Wall symbolized the threat to the peace of the World that was seen to come from the USSR. Even more amazing and dramatic has been the collapse of Communism in the Soviet Union and the division of the country into independent states.

The origins of the Curtain and the Wall

The Iron Curtain dates from the Second World War, when Stalin joined forces with the Allies to defeat Hilter and Nazism. The USSR had suffered dreadfully from the Nazi invasion in 1941. Stalin wanted a barrier between the USSR and Germany. As the Soviet forces moved westwards towards Germany, they made sure that 'friendly' governments were set up in eastern European countries (see map).

What they really meant were Communist governments. This alarmed the western powers, who saw this as the beginning of a Communist take-over. So, Europe became divided by this Iron Curtain.

Map showing the Iron Curtain in 1949.

NETH.
BELG.
LUX.
FRANCE
WEST GERMANY
SWITZ.
ITALY
Berlin
EAST GERMANY
CZECHOSLOVAKIA
AUSTRIA
HUNGARY
YUGOSLAVIA
ALBANIA
GREECE
POLAND
USSR
ROMANIA
BULGARIA
TURKEY

N

0 200 km

The Iron Curtai
Communist countries
Communist but not under USSF

When the war ended, the USSR refused to leave East Germany. Suspicion and hostility continued to grow in the post-war years. The USSR, the USA and Europe prepared for future conflict by building nuclear weapons. This period became known as the **Cold War**. In 1961, Khrushchev, the Soviet leader, ordered the building of a Wall across Berlin. No-one was allowed to move from east to west. It was ugly and frightening. It showed that Europe was divided between Communism and Democracy. When the Wall came down in 1989 it showed that the Cold War was coming to an end and that Communism was weakening.

The Berlin Wall in the 1960s.

The collapse of Communism

The destruction of the Wall can be explained by events in the USSR. In 1985 Mikhail Gorbachev became the new leader of the USSR. Gorbachev wanted peace and friendship with the West. Soviet citizens were given more freedom. They were allowed to travel and to make more contact with the West.

However, the final act in the drama took the World completely by surprise. In August 1991 a coup was attempted in Moscow by a group of hard-line Communists who wanted to stop Gorbachev's reforms whilst he was away on holiday. The coup was stopped by Boris Yeltsin. By the end of 1991, he had replaced Gorbachev as leader. The Communist Party officially ceased to exist. Statues and other reminders of the 1917 Revolution were attacked. The USSR was replaced by the **Commonwealth of Independent States** (CIS). Today the republics all have their own governments and presidents.

Time has yet to tell how the startling events of 1991 will work out. The independent states still struggle to survive by themselves. The people now have to develop a new sense of nationality for they are no longer citizens of the Soviet Union. They have also to come to terms with the truth about the past that has been hidden from them for so long. Historians will play an important role in this process. One thing is certain, the drama of the end of the USSR can only be matched by that of those 'Ten Days that Shook the World' in 1917.

Time Chart

1870	Lenin born at Simbirsk.
1894	Nicholas II becomes Tsar and marries Alix of Hesse (Alexandra).
1904–5	Russia defeated in the Russo-Japanese War.
1905	January: 'Bloody Sunday' in St Petersburg. Year of strikes and serious unrest (1905 Revolution).
	October: State Duma promised.
1914	Beginning of First World War.
1916	Rasputin murdered.
1917	February: Revolution following strikes and unrest in Petrograd. Tsar Nicholas II abdicates.
	October: Led by Lenin, the Bolsheviks carry out a second revolution in Petrograd.
1918	March: The Treaty of Brest Litovsk signed with Germany. Civil War begins.
	July: Tsar Nicholas II and his family executed at Ekaterinburg.
	Period of 'War Communism' – very unpopular.
1921	Famine in Soviet Russia. Mutiny of sailors at Kronstadt.
	Lenin introduced his New Economic Policy.
1924	Death of Lenin. Joseph Stalin becomes leader of the USSR. Communism is established in the USSR.
1939	Beginning of Second World War.
1943	Germany defeated at the Battle of Stalingrad.
1945	End of Second World War. The Iron Curtain comes down. The Cold War begins.
1953	Death of Stalin.
1961	The Berlin Wall is built.
1985	Mikhail Gorbachev becomes leader of the USSR.
1989	Berlin Wall comes down. End of the Cold War.
1991	Break up of USSR. Commonwealth of Independent States set up.

A note about dates:

Until February 1918, the old calendar was used in Russia. This was thirteen days behind the calendar used in Western Europe. The dates used in this book follow the old Russian calendar before February 1918.

Glossary

abdicate when a monarch gives up ruling a country.

absolute ruler a ruler who has complete power and runs a country without a parliament. Before 1917, the Tsar ruled Russia on his own. He was an **absolute monarch**.

Bolsheviks a group of people, led by Lenin, who wanted to overthrow the Tsar in Russia and bring in Communism. The Bolsheviks took power in Russia after the October Revolution of 1917.

Capitalism when private individuals are allowed to run their own businesses and factories.

Cold War a war of words between the western Capitalist world (led by the USA) and the eastern Communist world (led by the USSR). Each side was very suspicious of the other. The Cold War lasted from 1945–1989.

Commonwealth of Independent States came into being when Communist rule collapsed in the USSR in 1991. The USSR was disbanded. The republics which had made up the USSR came together and formed the CIS.

Constitutional monarch a monarch who has limited powers and rules with a parliament.

Cossacks cavalry soldiers from southern Russia.

Commissar name for a minister in the government in the USSR.

dissidents people who disagree with a government and speak out against it.

emancipation freedom from slavery.

Kremlin headquarters of the government in the USSR.

Mensheviks a group of people, led by Alexander Kerensky, who wanted to overthrow the Tsar. They wanted moderate changes in Russia.

Okhrana the Tsar's secret police.

Orthodox Church the main Christian church in Russia.

Provisional Government the government of Russia between March and October 1917. Took power after Tsar Nicholas II had abdicated. Its rule was ended by the Bolsheviks in the October Revolution.

purges between 1934 and 1938 Stalin carried out a campaign to get rid of anyone who he thought was against him. Millions were sent to labour camps or executed.

Reds name given to supporters of the Bolsheviks.

self-sufficient ability to supply all goods needed, without the help of other countries.

serf a person forced to stay and work on the master's land.

Soviet a council of workers and soldiers elected by the people.

Tsar title given to the Emperor of Russia.

Tsarevich title given to the eldest son of the Tsar.

Tsarina title given to the Empress of Russia.

tyranny when a country is under the control of a cruel ruler.

USSR Union of Soviet Socialist Republics, often shortened to Soviet Union. This was the name given to the Russian Empire after the Bolsheviks had taken power.

Whites supporters of the Tsar in the Russian Civil War.

Index